Letters From The Grave

Marie Cardinal

&

Louis Cartwright

Dedication

This book is dedicated to Robert and Elizabeth Cardinal with special acknowledgement to Bob Cardinal, Vincent Cardinal, and Kimberly Cardinal-Carbonaro . And a most special acknowledgement to Brian Sweeney who selflessly fixed my broken wings so that I may fly free.

Louis

Louis stabbed to death & I am in Bruges, Belgium.

Somehow I am having no let-up of activity. Still going on and wondering why if one of us had to die why not me? I was the older and it is more logical.

Regardless, I never had the thought Louis might be killed by someone on a New York City Street.

Attempt to grasp a kind of logical succession of events leading to the happening. Louis could infuriate to a state of anger; besides he had reached defeat.

So it went.

Louis is gone from my life

I loved him & I miss him immensely.

He will be part of me always.

It is and it will be, in a manner of speaking, sadness and the feeling of being aware of a sort of joy attached to the knowing of Louis of his friendship. He was extremely warm and loyal. No matter how one can speak of what our lives became together or apart. Knowing the end of his life also means the end of the friendship.

So be it.

Louis was my companion, my ace spoon buddy, my heart-held close close friend and so it goes.

- Herbert Huncke

Contents

Letters From The Grave

"Pull it tighter Galina." I could tell Galina was becoming frustrated with me. "It's as tight as it can go," she replied. It was my turn to help her gown up. In moments we would be entering the unit. The Covid-19 unit. We walked slowly toward the sealed tarp. I couldn't help but wonder why I signed up for these shifts. I wanted to run away, I was scared. I didn't. I unzippered the tarp and we walked through. Galina and I were the only nurses to care for forty-six patients. We received end-of shift report from the nurses we were relieving. We couldn't see their faces just their eyes. Fear in their eyes is what I saw. The nurses left the unit and Galina and I started the count on how many patients were affected by the deadly virus. All forty-six patients were positive. I heard the whistling of fans coming from the patient's rooms; as I made my rounds, I unplugged them all. All the patients had the same expression on their dying faces: anguish and fear. Death was not foreign to Galina and I, we were hospice nurses. We comforted people who were dying of natural causes. There was absolutely nothing natural about this plague. It attacked quickly and literally took the breath out of them. When I got back to the nurse's station I went through the charts. "Galina, no one is a DNR!" Galina looked back at me and in her thick Russian accent screamed,

"It's going to be a long night; grab the crash cart 206 is coding."

It was a long night. I was so relieved when I saw the on-coming nurses through the tarp. We gave a quick report and ran towards the exit. Once outside of the building, I pulled my mask off and took in several deep breaths of fresh air. The skin on my nose was torn and swollen. We stripped naked in the parking lot and doused ourselves in alcohol to remove any remnant of the plague. We slipped into our clean clothes and drove home. It was cold out but we had the windows down, letting the wind hit our faces. Galina drove in silence, I looked at her as she stared blankly at the road. I knew what she was thinking, I was thinking the same about how torturous it was for us to perform CPR on patients in their nineties. No families bedside, no one came but the funeral directors dressed as martians to pick them up. An hour later we reached my car parked in an empty Costco lot. As I was getting out of her car, I reached over and hugged her, "I love you, Galina." I meant it too. It was at that moment I understood the love soldiers had for one another.

I reached home and showered. I got into my bed and drifted off to sleep. When I woke up I saw the box on the table. It was from the N.Y. Foundling. I opened it and a bunch of letters came pouring out. They were all addressed to 'Kim.' In this moment of exhaustion, I remembered my name was Kim. I was Kim and these were letters from my biological father, Louis Cartwright. I had recently found my biological parents and I knew he was dead. The letters were a blessing from beyond. I put them back in the box, I was already running late for my next shift. Brian, my partner of twenty years, was calling me to the kitchen. "Come and eat the sandwich I made for you." I've known Brian since I was four years old. He was there when my adoption was finalized and my name was changed to Marie. I told him about the letters and said I would read them after I completed my shifts at the unit. Two months later I reached for the box safely secured in my closet. These are my letters from the grave.

Letter # 1

September 1972

To my baby Kim,

I I don't know what happened today. I was outside the courthouse waiting for your Mother. Today was a big day for us. I feared I was late until I saw the car pull up and you were gently taken out of the car and you were being led into the building. The man that held your hand looked wealthy, the woman that held your other hand was beautiful. I waited for hours and never saw your Mother. You came out again with the strangers that weren't strangers to you. They looked happy as they placed you back in their car. I was confused as to what was happening. You were being fostered and now you were adopted. Joyce told me that she was not signing the papers to let you go. We were going to try and make the family we made with you work. I hadn't had a drink in days. I'm hoping we didn't lose you, maybe you weren't being adopted and the court was postponed. But I know the system, we lost. I hope you remember us. I hope you remember your name. Your Mother didn't want the name Kim at first but I convinced her it was a strong name for you. I really named you after the beautiful Kim Novak. Joyce wouldn't have liked that so I left that part out when naming you. Today as the car pulled away, I ran after it and screamed, "Don't forget your name. Your name is Kim." I feel like a coward now. I waited for the car to pull off. In my heart I know you are gone. I now gave you a life that I led. I was adopted too. Your mother knew I didn't want any of my children in the system. What I didn't know at the time was your mother was a child. She lied to me. She told me she was my age and she wasn't. She was sixteen when she strolled into my friend's apartment. I was nineteen. I never thought about it. We did cocaine all night and she made me laugh. I saw her several times after that and one night I made her a line and she refused. That's when she told me she was pregnant and sixteen. I did her line and mine. I was going to be a father. I did a few more lines. I am going to go to her house and find out what happened to her and to you. I will write soon. Be strong like your name Kim. Be strong.

Yours,

Louis

PS: I hope you are in NY

Dear Louis,

Your letters have found me. Unfortunately, you are gone. When I received the box of letters I imagined them to be from Joyce, my mother. Never would have I expected they would be from you, my father. The day you wrote of was my adoption day. You did lose me. I spent my life looking for you and Joyce. Forty-three years I looked. I found you shortly before my forty-seventh birthday. You were forty-seven when you died. I just turned fifty-two when I received your letters to me. It saddens me that you didn't get to see the age of fifty. I have decided to write you back for each letter you have written to me. I feel as if I owe that to you, dead or not.

It was a Sunday morning when my DNA results came in. Weeks earlier I mustered up the courage to ask a man I found on Facebook to test with me. He had the same last name as Joyce. We resembled each other. It was a long shot. But, I was right, he was my first cousin. Born to the eldest brother of Joyce's. I sat and read the results. Another person showed up but from your side, an Aunt. I reached out to the man who tested for me. Kevin Indrieri. He answered his phone saying, "Well good morning cousin." I had a million questions. Kevin answered all but one. The most important one was not answered. Was my Mother alive? Kevin wanted to connect me with his father, my uncle. I had to wait for three painstaking days for my Uncle Richard to call me.

While I waited I messaged the mysterious 'Aunt' from your side. She messaged me back right away. We exchanged phone numbers and I called her. Before I could even ask who you were, she blurted out, "Your Father is Louis Cartwright." I googled your name quickly. As I read the words, she spoke them. "You're father was murdered in NY in 1994." I couldn't hear anything else. I stood staring at your picture that was online. I rushed her off the phone and started to cry. There you were on YouTube. You were a junkie and looked like one. I had waves of emotion. I wanted to call everyone I knew to tell them you were found, I didn't because I was ashamed. I didn't want to be, but I was. You had missing teeth and were thin and frail. Your voice was raspy and accent thick. I knew you were mine from the sunken eyes, I too had. You had big beautiful brown sad eyes. My eyes are blue and are just as sunken and sad as yours. When I heard your voice I was paralyzed. I knew you. I knew your voice. I watched and read all about you. In conversation with your sister, she told me you had famous friends. I looked each one up, and most of your friends did reach fame, I recognized William Burroughs and Allen Ginsberg. I was curious about the man referred to as 'Huncke'. I learned later it was Herbert Huncke; another junkie. A brilliant junkie.

Lost in thought, Brian arrived home and I shouted, "My father is Louis Cartwright, a murdered junkie on the lower east side. He's on YouTube. " Brian thought it was great. We watched you on YouTube together and Brian's excited reaction was all I needed. After saying to myself several times, "He was a murdered junkie." I became less ashamed. Brian went to bed and I spiraled into a deep dive of you and your friends. The famous friends were the original Beats from the Beat Generation. I went to bed praying Joyce was still alive.

Three days later the phone rang. It was Joyce's brother, Richard. He was so gentle in telling me, " I'm so sorry, your mother passed away in 2009." I missed her by eight damn years. We spoke for hours. Richard is one of the biggest blessings I have received to date. I didn't cry when we got off the phone. We made plans to meet in a few weeks. I was numb. Brian returned home and asked if he called. I said he did. "She's gone too, Brian. I have no living biological parents." Brian hugged me; he rarely did that. The hug was the acknowledgement that I found graves. We went to bed. I stared up at the ceiling and thought, "Fuck you, God, just fuck you." It wasn't until the morning when Brian left for work that I smashed every dish I owned. I cursed and screamed, " How did you take her God?" I threw my kayak into the freezing water and paddled out to the marshes and screamed again, "I was a good girl, I followed you, I prayed for one thing in life and you took her, you took them. Eight fucking years ago." That night I received a call from my biological sister, Mary. Joyce had her four years after me. She too was adopted and you were not her father. We also spoke for hours and planned to meet that week. That night I went to bed and said to God, "Okay big guy you are redeeming yourself. Thank you for sparing her."

That night you came to me in a dream. We were sitting on a bench. You were young and beautiful. All you said was, "Find me, Kim. The real me." You kissed my cheek and when I woke up my face was moist from the tears, or maybe from your kiss. More soon, off to work I go.

Yours,

Kim

PS: I stayed and grew up in NY

Letter #2

Sept 1974

My beautiful baby Kim,

We lost you. I went to your mother's house and was told she had the baby, your sister. What are the chances she would have the baby on that most important day? I waited a few weeks and waited down the street for Joyce to appear. But when she did I hardly recognized her. Joyce was so beautiful when pregnant with you and your sister. She was so full of life. But now this girl stood before me and her expression was blank. She was so thin. I asked what happened and she told me that she gave you both away. "A better life." I think that's what she mumbled. I asked her again if she was on drugs, she was so different. "Drugs? I wish. They gave me electric shock treatments." she answered. My mind was taken to a time in my life that I was desperately trying to forget. My adopted mother also had electric shock treatments. I asked her if she wanted to go for lunch. She said no. I pulled out my flask and offered her a drink. She took a swig then cried. Not knowing what to say I told her we could have another baby. She pushed me so hard and said, "Go away Louie, and don't ever come back again. Before you go give me the flask." I did what she asked. I walked away. I mouthed to her, "I love you." She mouthed back, "Drop dead." I will probably never see her again. I was leaving Brooklyn soon. My friend and I are moving to Manhattan. I looked back at her again. I did love her but I hated her too.

I'm sorry Kim. I hope your parents are good to you. I hope you are never in harm's way. I hope you have a better go at life than I did. I should have taken you and ran as fast as I could to Ohio. That's where I grew up. My sister has children and I could have left you with her. She hates me too though. You look like her. Like my sister Kathy. She has the perfect life and has no reason to hate me. I left Ohio because I had to. She stayed because she wanted to. We are so different, Kim. I have so much I want to tell you, so I am going to write to you. And if you get these letters you can write me back.

Yours,

Louis

PS: You are a Baptist. I hope you are raised in our faith.

Dear Louis,

To be honest you lost me long before the day you waited outside the courthouse. I was never coming back after I was fostered. I was adopted by Bob and Betty Cardinal. They had three biological children of their own and felt that they could help a child and expand their already-made family. They weren't wealthy but they were well off. They gifted me with two older brothers and a sister. I blended easily with the other children. I was truly thrown into the mix and was never meant to feel 'adopted.' I grew up in a middle class neighborhood and had all the delights of a privileged child. I was swimming in the swim club we belonged to and was vacationing in our summer home in the Poconos. I was never without my siblings. I attended a catholic school and was a Brownie. (I never made it to be a girl scout.)

Let's talk about you for a bit. You were born to Charles and Nellie Weekley. You had an older brother (James), when I say older I mean nine months older, and a sister (Kathy) a year younger than you. Charles and Nellie met in New Orleans while he was stationed in the Army. They married after two weeks and she was pregnant a few months later with James.

All seemed to be okay until Charles came home. He was different after having served in the Army. He was so handsome Louie. He was blonde with the most beautiful blue eyes and a winning smile. But he drank. He came back to a family of three children and was a drunk. Nellie had saved all the money she earned working as a waitress in a local diner in Ohio. Charles just wanted to drink. He squandered all the money and they were forced to live with his mother, your grandmother, Bertha.

The story told is that you and James were unruly and Bertha called Children Services and had the three of you hauled off to an orphanage. Both Nellie and Charles were charged with abandonment. James was adopted right away, I believe he was four at the time; you and Kathy stayed behind while Nellie frantically tried to get you back. Nellie's only crime was that she was poor. She remarried and had your youngest sister. A half-sister. That was who I first spoke to when my DNA results came back. You and Kathy were adopted by Melvin and Marge Cartwright. You were around six. Nellie tragically died at either 36 or 38 of Leukemia. I believe she died of a broken heart. Either way, you were all destined to be orphans with her passing so young.

Charles moved to Arizona and never had any more children. I feel very connected to Charles for some reason. In my mind growing up he would be the description of what I would have thought you looked like. When I first saw his picture, I placed it close to my heart and said, "In a world where you did not feel love, I love you, Charles." I feel like

Charles got duped in life with his miserable mother, the army, and the loss of his children. He worked for the railroad for 25 years in Arizona. He was advised to retire as he had put in the years, when he did they told him he retired six days too early and he did not receive his pension.

He drank in excess and one day fell and hit his head. He developed a brain hemorrhage and refused treatment. He was later found dead in his chair with a cold brew in hand. When I received his death certificate it stated he died of Alcohol. I never even knew that was a thing to state alcohol as a cause of death. I am currently requesting the state of Arizona to change that to Cerebral Hemorrhage. I will try to write again soon. This Covid plague is still rampant and I'm the busiest I ever have been at work.

Yours,

Kim

PS: I was raised and am Catholic, and thank God you did not leave me in Ohio.

Letter # 3

December 15th, 1974

My baby Kim, Can I still call you a baby? You are my big girl now at five years old. I think of you all the time. I called Joyce today and when she answered the phone and knew it was me she hung up. I waited again for her at the corner. She looks better Kim. We went for a walk and she told me that in order for her to move on I would have to stop calling her every time I wanted to remind her we lost a baby. The truth is I didn't lose a baby, she gave my baby away. She had no right to do that. How do we know you will have a better life? I think you belonged with us. I'm doing odd jobs and am writing. With the help of her mother, we could have made it. But then there's the part of me that thinks that what if we didn't make it and you were unhappy with us, knowing that you had a chance of a better life. That's how Joyce sees it. But I still feel resentment that I was led to believe you were coming home. Maybe that's why I write to you because I never got the chance to say goodbye. Joyce says I got more than she did, I saw you off. Why didn't I write the plate number down? Why didn't I scream out before they pulled off? Joyce thinks if I really wanted you I could have fought for you. Yet again a choice that wasn't viable. She was only sixteen when she got pregnant, I couldn't even sign the birth certificate without risking jail. I shouldn't even be writing to a five year old about this but I want you to know the truth always as I know it. We parted ways again today and she left me with all unresolved feelings Kim. I should have been a part of all of this.

I hope you are a happy five year old despite all we have done to leave you an orphan. I am so sorry. Stay strong Kim.

Yours,

Louis

PS: You smiled at me at two weeks old and wrapped your finger around a curl in my hair. I miss your smile more than you could ever know. I hope one day you will know how much we both loved you.

Dear Louis,

Firstly, I have to remember I am a middle-aged adult writing back to a twenty-five-year-old. I do agree with you that you should have been included in whatever concerned me. But you didn't change. You kept partying with your friends. I thought for a long time about why Joyce's mother didn't want to keep me. I was already in Christmas pictures, we were a family. Uncle Richard told me the truth. Joyce kept partying too. You weren't "meeting" on the corner, she was sneaking out her window. Her mother had buried her husband, my Grandfather a few years before she got pregnant. He died an awful death of Melanoma and even lost an eye. She became a nurse later in life and was supporting her own children. In many ways I was like Joyce. I never listened and snuck out my window to meet friends. Difference being she had a baby at home. Oh, and I wasn't on drugs. I think that made a difference too. I'm not blaming or judging you or Joyce but to want to leave me in Ohio with your sister or having my Grandmother raise me in Brooklyn weren't exactly parental ideas or solutions. I spent my life thinking I had it so hard. It was actually you who had it hard. I know all about your childhood. You had it pretty good up until you were fifteen. I'm waiting for the letter of you telling me what happened. Tell me Louis, why exactly did you "have" to leave Ohio? You blamed Joyce and she blamed you. I never blamed either one of you.

You didn't write the plate number down because you knew in your heart that I was going to a better place. I was going to be fed and sleep peacefully knowing where my next meal was coming from. You didn't scream out because you had nothing to bring to the table, you knew that the man that held my hand was the table. He was stable, you wanted me to be stable. You both had four years to pull it together. You didn't. At the end of the day your desire to be a father and being a father are two different scenarios. You are confusing the two.

I must admit that I am still a little mad that you wanted to take me to Ohio to be raised by Kathy. I would have resented you. Although she did move to a nice spot in Florida, always wanted to live in Florida. I found her Louie and she did hate you. More soon, I'm on call tonight and just got a call. I hate ending this letter because there is so much more to say. And I'm not an orphan.

Yours,

Kim

PS: When I first googled your picture I put my fingers on your curl, I'm smiling at you now. Come and kiss my cheek again in my dreams, please. And if you could maybe talk to the big guy up there and ask him to give us a damn break with Covid!

Letter # 4

December 15th, 1975

Dearest Kim,

I took your Mothers' advice to stop writing you. But this year I can't help myself. Things are going really well for me. I started writing a book. I went to Kabul and spent a few months journaling. I met some pretty crazy cats and am lucky to be alive. I'm taking photographs too. My friend Herbert thinks they are pretty good. I think so too.

I can't believe you are seven already. I think about the things you may be doing. I'm learning so much about writing. I wanted to be a writer or a journalist. It's very important to do the things that make you happy. Life will creep up on you. The world is in a state of craziness. We are in need of a change. I was raised Republican but share Democratic values. I don't really care about politics. My time in the Navy taught me all I needed to know. Did I ever tell you I was in the Navy? It's how I escaped Ohio but as soon as I joined I knew I was not cut out for the Navy. I respect a man in uniform. You wouldn't catch me out there fighting for God knows what. That's my Navy story.

Kim as you grow into a young lady I want you to be careful. Don't trust everyone, even the ones you think you can trust. People have a way of changing. As you develop you will be looked at differently. It can be a shock at first. And if you still look like my sister, you are absolutely beautiful. I just hope you don't have her personality, she's wicked. I saw her last year and all she does is scowl at me. She used to be so much fun but then our parents divorced and when that happened everything changed. It's like she blames me for their lives going wrong. I'm not going to lie, it was a rough time for us both. I hope your family has stayed together. I hope seven is a wonderful year for you. I'm not going to call Joyce today maybe it's better if she forgot what day it is.

Yours,

Louis

PS: Your mother did not forget your birthday. She just called me and accused me of forgetting. But we had some good laughs. She seems to be in a better place even withme.

Dear Louis,

I am going to share with you my experience with your sister Kathy. When I took the DNA test I matched with her. I sent a message but she never responded for a long time. The DNA kit was a gift for her and she wasn't in charge of the messages when they finally reached her, I was sort of done with all of this. I found so many people that I was overwhelmed with meeting someone else. But her son Mike called me and said she would definitely want to talk to me.

When she called me we both cried. Then we laughed because we didn't know why we were crying. Kathy is the only person that expressed her feelings and they were identical to mine. She understood my need to find you. She understood that even if one had the best family situation in adoption, one would still have the need to know where one came from. I booked a flight to Florida and thought of all the questions I wanted to ask her. When I reached Florida I drove to her and she was waiting on her lounger with Mike by her side. I was amazed at the likeness between her and me. I couldn't wait to see what I would look like in my seventies. I will admit menopause has taken its toll on me. The belly weight gain is awful. I was starting to be the same shape as Winnie the Pooh. So needless to say when she stood up and I saw Winnie the damn Pooh, I was disappointed. But not disappointed with her. We stayed up all night talking. I saw all your childhood photos. I saw all the places your adoptive parents took you. I was really confused. You looked to be such a happy boy. I was starting to feel like Kathy wasn't telling me something. I didn't push right away, I thought the next day I would ask her why I felt so off.

We went to bed at four am and at nine am she was standing in front of my bed all dressed up wanting to take me to breakfast. At breakfast, I told her I got all bitten up by mosquitos, "Oh no" she said, "You got bit by fleas, I have such a problem with them." Her trailer was infested with fleas and I had another night to get attacked by them. Breakfast went well. She asked me about my life and I saw a sadness in her when she told me about the divorce. When she told me that Marge had two biological children a few years after adopting you I started to piece it together. Kathy told me that Marge played a mean game of divorce and accused Melvin of sexually abusing Kathy. I felt a lump in my throat and softly asked, "Did he abuse you?" "NO!" she shouted. I knew then she was lying. We went home to rest before dinner with Mike and I knew there was so much more going on than I was being told. I wasn't sure I wanted to know.

Dinner was so much fun. Mike was great and I was to meet his twin brother Rick the next morning before my flight home. That night Kathy had a cocktail, she hadn't had a drop since Her husband died, ten years earlier. Mike and I bid her a good night and we hit the bars. We drank and danced until the sun came up. When he dropped me off, I crawled into bed with Kathy and put my arms around her and whispered in her ear, "I know you were hurt Aunt Kathy and I'm sorry." She embraced me and she fell back asleep. I was woken up by the crackles in her breath sounds. I laid there thinking, Fuck, you have cancer, I just know it. That morning I met Rick and his wife. We had so many laughs, it was easy to be around them. I knew I was coming back to meet her daughter Tammy in a month, I thought it best to leave her alone with all the questions for then.

When I returned to NY I started researching you again and to my surprise, an article about David Wojnarowicz came up and the interviews he did with you were in an archive at Columbia University. When I arrived at the University to hear the cassette tapes I wasn't expecting to hear what I did. Your voice was soft and I could hear the crack in diction when you told David in an interview that you had a bad start in life, that you were rescued by the Cartwright's but everything changed when your mother found you masturbating. You said she "finished you off." and that you wanted to die after that night. That your life in Ohio was over. When you applied to Ohio State she told you that the money saved for education was not for you and Kathy but for her "boys." That's why you joined the Navy. Now I understood Louie the junkie.   After listening to the tapes I excused myself and asked for a bathroom. I threw up several times and thought of stealing the tapes. I didn't. I placed them back in the box and left. I hit the nearest bar and got drunk. I called Kathy and told her what I discovered. She had no idea but also realized that you started to change at that time. I asked her again about Melvin and she wept and said, " He was a good man, Kim, he was under so much pressure and was being accused of it and he lost himself one night and called me into the garage, he only kissed me on my mouth and did some fondling." She went on to defend his honor. Is that why you warn me about how people can change? Is that why you were scared of putting me in the system? I left the bar and headed home. I had to pull over several times and vomit. I pulled into a rest stop and looked in the mirror and said aloud, " You are one lucky girl. " My brothers and my Father, Bob, never looked at me other than a daughter and a sister. It never entered my mind that I could have been sent to a home and could have been raped or "fondled." I mean I know it happens but I never thought of it ever in my case. I was all of sudden extremely grateful that my ass was beaten with a belt and nothing else.

When I went to Florida the second time to meet Tammy she told me how mean Kathy was when raising her and the twins. I could go into detail but it's not my story to tell but do know that you are absolutely correct that I would have been resentful to have been dumped off in Ohio. I adore Tammy and we have become very close. More soon.

Yours,

Kim

PS: I was happy to read Joyce was in a better place. Also, I know you were thrown out of the Navy for getting the whole crew high on Opium. The Navy dropped you off in San Francisco and that's where you met Allen Ginsberg and went back to NY with him.

Dear Louie,

I couldn't sleep and my thoughts are racing. Shortly after my discovery at Columbia, I again returned to Florida. Kathy was dying of cancer. A few days before my flight she told Tammy I was coming. She knew I would come and be there for them. She knew she was dying. She spent a few weeks lying to us that she was going for treatment, Tammy knew she wasn't, we all knew she was lying. She declined quickly and there was a tumor bursting out of her armpit. For comfort reasons, the doctors were to perform surgery. Kathy could have made things right with her children, she only favored Mike. Yet it was her daughter who took care of her. I was surprised she didn't use her last opportunity to clear up loose ends. She didn't.

When I arrived she was already taken to the Hospice house and put on comfort medications. I touched her hand and her eyes opened and she said, "You did come for me." It was only the third time I was meeting your sister, Louie and I knew my part was to help her cross over. I told Tammy to tell her anything she needed to. Tammy sat with her and told her that she forgave her and knew the cruelty she showed her growing up had nothing to do with her. It was all the pent-up anger Kathy had that she took out mainly on Tammy. Kathy was blessed to have a daughter who wanted nothing but love from her mother. Tammy got nothing.

As Kathy took her last breath, her eyes opened wide and she softly said, "Louie." I knew you were her gatekeeper. After Kathy died it was revealed that Kathy left everything to Mike. Even in death, Kathy was cruel to her children, knowing the money would separate the boys and hurt Tammy. Shortly after Kathy died, Mike did too. He too was diagnosed with cancer and within a few months, he joined his mother and his nasty girlfriend walked away with all of Kathy's inheritance. What a shame. I hope the two of you sorted all your stuff out and are basking in the reward of God. I remain close to Tammy and will always be by her side to pick up the pieces of her shattered heart. Mike's death has devastated her; I'm thankful she married a good man to take care of her. I will hold the time I had with Kathy as precious but I am eternally grateful I pulled off with the Cardinals that day in 1972. The thought of Kathy raising me still sends chills down my spine.

Yours,

Kim

Letter #5

December 15th, 1980

My beautiful girl Kim,

The big twelve today! Happy birthday! I just celebrated my thirty-second birthday and I feel like it's time to settle down. Herbert and I are always on the go and I'm feeling tired. I've been traveling throughout Europe writing. I finally came up with the name of my book. I will title it 'Morpheus.' Herbert and I are getting quite serious about our art. I went home for Thanks giving and it was awful. I tried to clean out and I became quite ill. My mother is not well mentally and my father has taken up with an awful woman. I couldn't lift my head up for days. I finally got back on the bus to NY. I realized my home is here and I shouldn't return back to Ohio. I thought about enrolling in college. I don't think I have it in me anymore. It seems that that dream is no longer anything more than a dream. I went down the street and went to church. I'm not fond of Catholic priests; I see them in the bars luring young men into taxis after feeding them alcohol for hours, but the churches are beautiful and I find peace sitting alone and praying. I brought Herbert once but all we did was laugh because we were high. I now go alone in order not to be thrown out.

I met your mother the other day for dinner. We ate and drank for hours. I couldn't believe how much fun she was and we really had the time. When I was walking her home she told me she was in love and plans to marry some guy she has been seeing. She also told me that there is a possibility she will leave New York with this man because he is a Merchant Marine. I was happy until she said she might leave. Maybe she sensed my sadness because Kim she did the unthinkable. She held my arm in hers as we walked. I asked her what about Kim. She slid her hand in mine and asked, "Was she even real Louie?" We sat down on a park bench and I went over the events of the day the other family took you to their home to be their baby. For the first time, Joyce asked me questions. She asked if you were smiling, I told her you were. You actually didn't look happy at all getting into the car but no point in having Joyce know that. But I did tell her about the other children. Joyce knew of them and that's when I got angry. "How long was she with this family Joyce? How did you know the family had other children? I saw she was getting nervous but demanded answers. I finally screamed at her, "Do you know where she is Joyce?" She looked at the ground and said, "I think Staten Island." "Do you know where Joyce? Do you realize she lives in a damn dump, no one wants to live in Staten Island." Your mother swore up and down she didn't know who or where. I don't believe her Kim. I think she knows exactly who has you. I left her feeling awful and screamed at her that I better never find out she knew more than she told me. Walking home I thought maybe Staten Island wasn't so bad, it had less crime than the other boroughs and Snug Harbor was quite beautiful. I was hoping you were being raised in Upstate NY. I vow on this very day to never lay eyes on your mother again.

Yours,

Louis

PS: I did look back and screamed, "She was NOT smiling getting into the car!" I saw the look of horror on her face and feel vindicated.

Dear Louis,

That book you were writing you only got half done. It was awful. Some parts were funny and you certainly could tell a story but on a whole it was awful. I thought about finishing it for you but it was too little to work with. I was happy that in my research of you that you started writing short stories and a few got published and you made some money off it. I was also quite impressed to learn that you and Herbert went to local clubs and told stories and got paid for that as well. I found your book and the flyer you and Herbert had to advertise your performances in your friend's apartment. Jeremiah Newton. Jeremiah's story is for another letter but I have so much of yours from him. You truly had the most amazing friends.

Interesting view on the priests. Oddly enough when I was twelve the priest at the catholic school I was going to gave me my first alcoholic beverage and a cigarette. He would take a group of us in the woods and introduce us to different alcohol. That's where my love for vodka emerged. Things were getting rough for me from twelve on. I should have been in therapy. I often thought about running away. Looking back it's not as bad as my mind made it out to be. But it was still a rough time. I don't think I bonded properly with my adoptive mother and father. My mother didn't know how to handle me because I was so different in behavior than her other children.

It really all came from the trauma of the adoption. I remember Joyce. I remember a young slender tall girl with long brown hair and brown eyes saying goodbye to me. She told me she would be back for me. The Cardinal's verify that at one point in the adoption, they were scared because Joyce did change her mind. Maybe she really didn't know them. However, the address of where Bob grew up and where Joyce grew up is an eerie coincidence. You and Joyce had such a tumultuous relationship; it's harder to keep up with the love than the hate. She does fall in love. More to come on that. I know you resolve your conflicts with one another so on that note, I'm going to move on about Staten Island.

I must admit that your letters bring me back to the best memories of my childhood, I thank you for that. Staten Island was an amazing place to grow up. Although I became a chain- smoking, alcoholic in a catholic grammar school, I had the best foundation to education. More importantly my exposure to the friends I made then and still have today. If I wasn't raised in Staten Island I wouldn't have Brian. The young Brian took a beating for me in the fifth grade; I had my first kiss with the first love of my life, Patrick. Who by the way told me just a month ago he doesn't remember that life-changing kiss. I laugh at these memories. Staten Island was the best. We were members of the local swim club, I was on the swim team and dive team, and summers were split between the swim club and our summer home in the Poconos that my father built. I loved to feed deer and walk barefoot on the hot pavement; I can still taste the honeysuckle every-time summer approaches.   Twelve was an awful year for me. It's the year my spirit broke. My mother decided that I was too immature to move on to the eighth grade and I was left back. When I repeated the grade I was told that I would have to repeat the grade again due to immaturity. It was awful. How was it legal to leave any child back that never failed a test? I decided that the second time I would be unruly, those bastards at the school expelled me in May so that I would have to repeat the seventh grade a third time in public school. I can't even write about those three years I have them blocked from my mind. The only good thing for me during that time was my friendship with my public school friend Patty. I could have driven home from my eighth- grade graduation. I went one day to high school and left. I set out on foot to look for Joyce. I went to the Foundling and was turned away. Those were my worst years. I left the Cardinals a few years later. Through it all I still wouldn't change the adoption day and who I rode off with because of my sister Kim (hence my name change to Marie). Kim is my best friend and biggest supporter.

Yours,

Kim

PS: The story goes that when I was getting into the car that day, I was mad because Bob was putting my little suitcase in the trunk of the car, he said I kicked him and said, "Give me my stuff." Once I had my only possessions in life in my sight, I was fine. I wasn't scared to go with them, I knew them well. I loved the blue suit I was dressed in (all Betty's doing) and we went to feed the ducks that day at Historic Richmond town. It was a day of celebration. I just didn't know that it was the last day I would ever see the two of you again.

Letter # 6

June 4th 1982

Dearest Kim,

Your Mother got married today. What a beautiful bride. She married a really handsome dude too. I only went to the church because I wanted to take pictures for you. You are almost eighteen and will want to see these one day if you find us. Well, that was a mistake. She was walking down the aisle and saw me and the look she threw me, I should be dead right now. I kept snapping away. So don't mind the angry expressions they were directed towards me. But she was so beautiful, I cried some tears. I also cried tears when she met me outside and stepped on my foot. I told her the pictures were for you, then she smiled. "You really would have made a good Dad Louie, but it takes more than love." "Does he know Joyce? I won't tell but does he know?" "Yes" she replied, "He knows about Kim." "He wants children, Louie. I am going to be pregnant again soon. I want this chance to be a mother." I would want to report that I was mad when she said that but honestly, I want more children too. Please don't be hurt by that. I hope you love the pictures.

Yours,

Louie

PS: Eight days until I march in Central Park, I am marching to end nuclear disarmament and the Cold War arms race. We are facing very serious changes in America. I hope you travel outside of America, the world is a beautiful gift. But they are really messing around with nuclear bombs, it will destroy Earth and all of us in it.

Hi Louie,

I loved the pictures, even the angry ones. Uncle Richard gave me a photo album with all Joyce's pictures growing up. But I framed the two you sent me. Thank you, besides the photo album this was one of the most precious gifts I have ever received. Joyce was wrong, the love would have been enough. The marriage doesn't last though. Joyce does leave NY and moves to Virginia. She has the chance to become a mother again and had my two brothers, Patrick and Thomas. Things don't go as planned Louie. Joyce develops MS and lives the remainder of her life in a nursing home. Sadly, she dies alone in a VA hospital of Sepsis. The handsome dude divorces her in the nursing home and marries her best friend. They live in Florida and get drunk for Taco Tuesday, word on the street is he's not allowed back in for Tacos on Tuesday any longer.

I'm happy you went to see her.

Yours,

Kim

PS: Good for you for marching. Nuclear bombs are still a threat.

Letter # 7

December 15th 1982

Hi beautiful,

You are fourteen already. Four more years and you will receive these letters. I know we will be together. I plan on spending a few months in India, I'm leaving in a few days. Then I will come back and spend the summer upstate. The city isn't the safest place to be right now. Herbert is working on his book now and I haven't really been writing, I've been so busy taking photos. My friend Bill has been a big help in getting me gigs. I've started a bank account. My first one in years. I deposited 325 dollars in it yesterday. I have to go back to Ohio and I dread it but I need to renew my license. I don't know why I bother, I never drive. I've cleaned up, Kim. I'm dry and more creative than ever. I wonder if you write at all. I wonder what your desires are. I hope you are the happiest you have ever been because after eighteen the world is yours and hopefully mine.

Something terrible is happening and not only in NY. There is a disease lurking around and they are calling it the gay man's disease. That's what they want us to believe. So many of my friends are dying. I think it's the way to eradicate homosexuals. The horror of the disease is bad enough but all infected are being treated like Lepors. It's really bringing me down. It's the reason I dried up. They say you can get it by sharing needles. I don't ever share my needles. I'm not sharing my straws anymore either. If it's a gay man's disease, why are children getting it? The disease is called AIDS.

I have not heard from your mother in a few months. I'm staying away. I think our time together has ended. I'm at peace with her and I feel she knows she can always come to me if needed. I'm not with anyone at the moment. I don't think I will ever fall in love. I hope you do. But not too soon, get your studying done first. Happy Birthday,

Kim!

Yours,

Louie

PS: I made you a painting. I'm painting now too.

Dear Louie,

I'm still in the seventh grade! I won't get these letters for a few more decades. That's the part in all of this that kills me. I went to the Foundling and they just wouldn't tell me anything. I know you are waiting for me and I can't even imagine your heartbreak when I don't come. Unfortunately, you will lose more friends. You will die not knowing that they have medication and some stay HIV positive only. The children got it from blood transfusions. You will fall in love Louie, hang in there, things get better before they get worse. The world is in no better shape. We are being forced to get vaccinations in the health field and I was really scared to take it. I was so sick after.

I do fall in love several times. I never give all of myself because I know nothing lasts forever. I can only depend on myself in life. I work a lot. That always was a factor in all my relationships. I never wanted children and that was a problem as well. I dated many older men because they required less of me. I wasn't like other girls in the sense that I wasn't dreaming of the big day. Brian is the only man that I moved in with. I can absolutely count on Brian. He's more than a partner, he is my best friend. We are going through a rough patch right now. I'm never home and when I am I don't think I'm present. We have been together now for twenty years and I've put him through hell and back. I tell you this because in an interview Herbert describes you as not allowing anyone to get too close to you either. We are more alike than I realized. Yours, Kim PS: Your painting is in my closet. Your friend Jeremiah gave it to me. I'm happy you didn't give up photography to become a painter.

Yours,

Kim

PS: Your painting is in my closet. Your friend Jeremiah gave it to me. I'm happy you didn't give up photography to become a painter.

Letter # 8

June 1986

Kim,

I have something to tell you and I want you to know it's hard for me to write this letter. I met a woman and we really hit it off. We just had a baby. A baby girl. I named her Halley after the comet. She is so tiny and beautiful like you were. Things aren't going well with her mother now and I'm under pressure. I told everyone about her, even my family back in Ohio. I want to do things differently this time. I called your Mother and told her about Halley and she was really happy for me. She also had a son and is pregnant again, hoping for another boy. I told her how guilty I felt and she said not to be. She also said, "Louie, I don't believe she will ever receive your letters. But if she does, we have something to offer her. She will have siblings." Herbert said the same thing. I don't want you to think we just forgot about you though. I'm waiting for December to come.

I'm writing poetry now in addition to photography. Herbert has been helping me. I'm taking the cover for Herbert's book that he just finished. We have been really busy and I even started acting. I think of what I had planned for my life and what has actually panned out for me and for the first time I am happy. I even went to a few therapy sessions to get my mind straight. My friend David has helped me sort through some of the stuff that happened to me in Ohio. I shock myself that I am able to be so straight with David. I consider him to be one of my best friends. Herbert is my family. You and Halley are my family too.

I love you,

Louis

PS: I'm writing a poem for you. If you do get these letters Kim and you don't want to know me please write back so I know you are okay. Please let one of us know you are ok.

Dear Louis,

I rolled my eyes at this letter. Let me grab a cocktail, roll a blunt, and we can break this down.

Okay so remember in the beginning I told you about the "mysterious Aunt?" That is your half-sister. Her name is not important. When we spoke she told me about Halley. I looked Halley up on Facebook and OH MY GOD, my heart sank. I spent an hour looking at her photos. She is me. In one photo I thought she was me. She has more striking features than I do and blessed be she did not inherit our double chins. She has our beautiful hair and our love for travel.

I sent her a message saying who I was and how I was a nurse and that I would love to meet her. I told her I appreciated her love of travel and that I had already conquered thirty countries. I told her we could travel to Paris and have a cocktail under the Eiffel Tower. Nice message, right? Wrong. She blocked me! I had her number and I texted her. Your daughter texted me back that she had girlfriends that were her sisters and had no interest in having me as her sister. She said she only traveled with a friend and that friend paid for it or something like that. She said she was in school and didn't need the distraction.

I'm not going to lie, I didn't handle the situation well, I called your half-sister back and asked her why she was like that. Your half-sister's dumb response was "Well that's the way it goes." I had already caught this half-breed sister in three lies, I never spoke to her again. She told me she didn't have children, that was a lie too. She didn't give me Kathy's information or help me find anyone but Halley and I think she knew Halley would react like that. What a sick bitch. Halley and I texted a few more times, and she said we could start slowly communicating by text. Then she never answered me again. In our few exchanges we had, she told me she didn't touch alcohol or any drug and her mother would be mortified if she knew I existed. That's when I knew she was damaged too.

I later found out that a 'friend' of yours kept in touch with her. We will call him 'J'. You knew J only a few years before your death. A grifter indeed. He followed Herbert Huncke around like a hemorrhoid. You died before he swindled the literary executorship of Huncke. I say swindled because there were far more important people in Herbert's life that Herbert would have trusted with his life's work. Then one day going through your boxes I found a letter from Herbert to Janine P. where Herbert is asking for her advice on what to do with his work. He hints that a man named Raymond Foye is his choice. I'm not saying J wasn't a friend but he was not the choice. Jeremiah told me that when

Herbert supposedly signed it for J to receive his life's work, J came excitedly running from Herbert's hospital room "I got it. I got it." That seemed strange to me. Everyone who surrounded Herbert Huncke claimed their love for him but he died alone. He died two years, two months, two hours after you. You both spent decades together and died alone. And J has done absolutely nothing with the great works of Herbert Huncke, instead he left it all in someone's house in France who no longer will speak to him. What a disgrace. Out of all the books I have read of Allen Ginsberg and William Burroughs, I think Herbert Huncke's books are the best. I just don't understand why J friended Halley. But I no longer care. She got stuck with the one friend of yours that I would think you would have not wanted in her life. I got gifted with the rest of your friends who are wonderful.

As far as Halley, I am always open to a relationship. But I don't need a sister either. I have my Kim. The sister I don't have to beg to see or receive love from. So sad that Halley wouldn't want to reap all the love I have to give. Or the vacations we will never take. But Louie, I know how much you love her and I would never turn her away. Anything I received that was yours, I keep half for her. Before I knew she didn't want a relationship I went and bought her the most beautiful sapphire and diamond evil eye. I wear it now everyday in hopes she changes her mind.

I love you too,

Kim

PS: If you knew where Herbert Huncke's remains lay you would die another death.

William S. Burroughs, Allen Ginsberg & Herbert Huncke
ca. 1975 by Louis Cartwright

Letter # 9

December 15th, 1987

Kim,

You are now nineteen now. I don't know if you are dead or alive. Again, your mother told me that you never received these. Maybe it's for the better. I'm not seeing Halley much these days either. I don't have any money to give her. Maybe she is better off too.

My friend Peter died. He was a photographer, like myself. Herbert and I saw him right before he passed and he looked awful. We are heartbroken. He died of AIDS. I don't think David will ever be the same. Peter had real talent and was an amazing person. He didn't deserve such a cruel death. David really looks bad these days. What more can I say, you aren't here, I feel lost. Halley is lost. My family is gone and Herbert is aging. What will I become when Herbert leaves the earth. Where will I go? Who will care that I was ever here at all. My letters to you are more now my journal to the daughter I will never see again. I wanted you here to be by me, but you are an adult now and I have nothing to offer you. Or maybe I do, I can offer you friendship if you are scared of anything more. I can also offer you my last name now.

Please write back.

Yours,

Louie

PS: I dream about you.

Oh, Louie,

I feel your desperation and it makes me nervous. And I know the ending. But hang in there sweetie, I promise there's a reward for you before you depart. I have some good news for you. I am going to make you an author. I am going to write a book with you as the co-author. I will title it, "Letters From The Grave." I tell people my story and yours and they seem interested, so why not? I will admit before your letters I started writing a book about how I found you and Joyce. I purged all the horrible events in my life that I guess I needed to. I want you to know by getting to know the real Louis Roy Cartwright, I healed. My inner child has healed. I know now you and I are bonded by trauma. I had an attachment disorder with my parents, I purposely rejected any and all positive relationships because it was me waiting for you and Joyce. I am not[unclear] you weren't healed of the trauma bonds you were haunted by the last generation. I am not blaming you, I am understanding you.

I did apply for a name change. I wanted to give that to you. The day of the courts, I stood in front of the judge and couldn't do it. How could I? On the way there a flood of memories took over my mind and my heart. I could remember, the Valentine's Day cards and gifts. I remembered the special birthday meals cooked by my mother, paid for by my father. I remember the rainy and cold nights they both ventured out to jobs to support us. I remembered Thanksgiving with my favorite Aunt and uncle. I remembered my cousins and how they loved me and I loved them. I apologized to the will continue to love my uncle Richard and his beautiful wife Christine. I have enough love but I will not walk away from who I am. Who I really am. You helped understand what abuse really looked like.

I'm sorry I couldn't save you. I'm sorry that your abuse reached the center of your soul and you allowed the demons of drugs and alcohol to rob you of a life. And really Louie, you loved the life as you led it. You couldn't sacrifice. Yes, you would have shown me love but I know the love you had for Herbert was your security. You could not have led both lives. It wasn't possible to be a junkie and a dad. You chose the life you wanted and I am choosing the one I want. You gave me back all the good I have experienced in life. The memories I shelved years ago. That to me is the best Father daughter gift you could have ever given me. I love you so much.

Yours,

Kim

PS: You come to me in my dreams. Come again soon.

Letter #10

December 15th, 1990

My daughter, Kim,

I have been in love for over a year now. She is the most beautiful girl in the world. Her name is Helen Oliver. She will become one of the greatest painters that lived. I have been going back to Ohio to maintain my Social Security benefit, I'm trying to get Halley some money and some for myself and Herbert. We are working on a few projects that will tide us over. We are in good company and have lots going on.

I hope you are well and your twenty-second birthday was a fun one. My birthday just passed on the eighth and I spent the day with Herbert and the night with Helen. Helen and her brother, Edgar are people Herbert and I really trust. Herbert is always saying, "Don't mess this up, Louie, she's a winner." I don't plan to.

Other than being in love, I am writing short stories and still taking photographs. My skills as a writer and a poet have vastly improved with the help of Herbert. When back in Ohio I gave my sister Kathy a box and told her to keep it no matter what. Some of my journals are in there and negatives that I just can't afford to develop right now. I put the poems I have written to you in there as well. I had a dream the other night that I was going to die. A woman who I knew but wasn't familiar with was in the dream as well. I was in a puddle of my own blood. I woke up gasping for air. I have been having a lot of nervous feelings lately. Maybe because my life is good right now. I'm always waiting for the bad luck to come.

I spoke to Joyce the other day, she hasn't been feeling very well. Last time she was in NY we met up for drinks at the bar. The more drinks we had the more we laughed but as always she turned angry with me. The last thing she said that night was for me to, "drop dead." I finally told her I am going to die soon and then she will be sorry. But I take Joyce in stride now, she called me the next day and we were laughing again. She really only gets nasty when she is drunk.

Yours,

Louie

PS: They say that you say the things you mean when you are drunk, Joyce does want me to drop dead, I think.

Dear Louie,

Haha, no she doesn't want you to drop dead. Or maybe she did, I don't know for sure. Louie in these next few years you will be your happiest with Helen and she does depart as your lover but Helen remains a true friend who loved you and you know that right up until you die.

In one of the many dreams you appear in, one night you were telling me that I wasn't looking in the right direction and you threw a penny at my foot. As you were leaving you handed me a bag full of Pennies and disappeared into the night. I was already in contact with your friend Jeremiah and the next time I went into the city, I told him about the dream. He laughed loudly and said, "I don't know why but Louie wants you to talk to Penny Arcade." Before I get into Helen and Penny, I have to tell you about Jeremiah.

My time with Jeremiah was very special to me. Jeremiah was easy to find. He came up in an article as your friend and the man who gave you his family plot in Calvary Cemetery in Queens, NY. When I read that you were not scattered in Potter's field, I cried, loudly. I just assumed you would be in the field due to the manner in which you lived and the circumstances surrounding your death. I messaged Jeremiah on Facebook with no reply. I then reached out to a friend of his and she passed the message on for him to call me. He did.

We talked for a few minutes and made plans to meet later that week. Jeremiah, to date, is the most interesting friend of yours.

When I reached Alphabet City in NY, I rode the elevator up and didn't know what to expect. I had read up on Jeremiah and he was well known for keeping the life and memories of Candy Darling alive. I became obsessed with Candy. When I reached his apartment he yelled for me to enter. Jeremiah had the same problem as many aging New Yorkers. He was outliving his small apartment and his 'things' had taken over. There was very little space to walk around. I assessed his situation and knew his most urgent need was a bed. I drove home that night in awe of Jeremiah and how many things of yours were saved by him. When I returned home I told Brian all about him and Brian said, "Here's my credit card, order him a bed." That was the start of what I thought would be an everlasting friendship.

Later that year Jeremiah became ill. I had no knowledge that he had been in the hospital and left a message on his door to call me. When he was discharged from the hospital he called. I immediately went to him. He was in awful shape. He was on the brink of losing it all. His rent was in arrears and he needed a significant amount of medical help if he wished to remain in his apartment. At the time I was working as a community health nurse and I knew I could help him but not alone. I looked up a handful of friends that he had on Facebook and reached out to them about his dire situation.

The only one that responded was Penny. The infamous Penny Arcade. I had known about Penny growing up. What New Yorker didn't? When she called, she was direct to the point as she was rehearsing for a show she was performing later that month at Joe's Public Theater. I was immediately impressed with Penny and her readiness to help Jeremiah. We spoke late into the night and devised a plan of care for him. I went to sleep that night relaxed knowing Jeremiah would be okay.

The next morning I called Jeremiah to let him know Penny would be helping and he was so happy his old friend cared. Then he went on to tell me that he had just hung up with a very nice lady who was also going to help him and she was coming later that morning to meet him. "In the apartment? She's coming to your apartment?" I shouted to him. "Where was she from Jeremiah?" Jeremiah not being nervous at all that he could be letting the wrong people in and delusional about his living conditions answered, " I think she said APS." The blood rushing from my face, I hung up on him and called Penny. When Penny answered I screamed, "Run, Penny run to Jeremiah's, Adult Protective Services are on their way". Penny sprinted into action and reached

Jeremiah with minutes to spare. He was being loaded into an ambulance as the 'Nice APS worker' arrived. I showered and headed to NYC. Penny and I knew he was only safe from eviction and placement to a nursing home for a short time. We went back to his apartment and we gasped at the task we had ahead in order to bring Jeremiah home.

The next day I quit my job to focus only on Jeremiah. I had to in order to bring him home in a safe, clean environment with home health services in place. I worked for weeks to get it done. It was a physical task and Brian also took time off to help us with painting, and getting the new floors installed. I paid his rent up to date, bought him another bed and he came home. When he saw the apartment he fainted. Honestly, he seriously fainted. It was empty. Jeremiah rushed me to get him home and his belongings that were salvaged were in storage. But in order to comply with the Fire Marshall I had to throw away a lot of books. I rid the apartment of books that were doused in cat urine and were mostly about how many different ways to make Pierogies. It took a few more monthsof Jeremiah bleeding my pockets dry and then he accused me of stealing all his books and other items that had fecal waste from cats on it. I swear, I knew as a nurse that these things happen but I never imagined how far gone Jeremiah was. He truly believed he had the most wonderful apartment and was surrounded by his most loved materialistic items. The Health Department would deem that differently.

Once he had the services he needed to stay home, he dumped me. Told me never to call him again. Although tempting because I really cared for Jeremiah, I have never called him again. But I don't regret my time with him because through Jeremiah I met so many important people that were in your life. Jamie Rasin, Laki Vazakas, and so many more people have become important in my journey to find you.

You and Herbert acted in a short film titled, 'The Burning Ghat.' It was award-winning and was an official selection of the Venice Biennale and was part of the Whitney Museum's "Beat Culture and the New America". You did that Louie!

Jamie went on to be the filmmaker of "Beautiful Darling: The Life and Times of Candy Darling, Andy Warhol Superstar."

He did this project with Jeremiah and it was recognized by MoMA and the Film Society of Lincoln Center. Laki was also very important to seek out. It was Laki, also a filmmaker, who followed you and Herbert around. He later debuts his film, 'Huncke and Louis.' Laki sent me a copy and I treasure it. His film allowed me into the broken parts of your life. I see your daily life and it's raw. It was hard to watch as a daughter but as a nurse, I understood that at the end of your life, you were in a spiraling state of psychosis. Drugs and alcohol didn't help, to see you paranoid and psychotic, feeling hopeless, made me celebrate your untimely death by the end of the film. Most importantly, Penny. I might not have reached out to Penny or known to if Jeremiah didn't recognize the sign you delivered to me in my dream. Penny has introduced me to the most fabulous people. Artists galore. Two artists I have come to love: Regina Bartkoff and Charlie Schick. Regina did the cover of this book. It's hard to imagine my life before any of these people. Those pennies you threw also led me to Edgar and Helen Oliver. Both are successful in the arts. I was most excited to meet them. You really did love Helen. Helen has spent hours with me remembering and sharing with me the love you two experienced. I'm feeling very blessed right now Louie. Those pennies were blessings coming my way. And thank you for throwing in Dean Lance. Dean filled me in on the Halley years when you fell in love with her Mom. All of these people filled in pieces of your puzzled life for me. All I can do is wish Jeremiah well.

Yours,

Kim

PS: I also say mean things when I'm drunk and not everything I say, I mean.

Letter # 11

January 11th, 1991

Dear Kim,

I am leaving to Belgium next week. I will arrive back in NYC in May of this year. I am writing again and still taking photos whenever opportunity presents. NY is becoming so dangerous to even step out on to the streets. Riots all over NY for one injustice or another. I went back to Ohio for Christmas and had a horrible time as always. I had to listen for hours about the Hubble telescope launching and more wars on the rise from Melvin. He has no idea what is actually happening in the world. He only thinks he does. I told him about what is happening in NY and told him about my friends dying of AIDS, he just looked in horror and said, "I question the life you have chosen Louie." He asked me about Halley and I made up a story to why I didn't bring her. I went down in the cellar and drank for the next three days then caught the bus back to NY. Ohio is more dangerous for me than NY in so many ways.

I think about you all the time these days. Who you are? Where you are? I talked to your mother the other day and she told us that a mutual friend of ours died in Brooklyn. I can sense that something is very wrong in Joyce's life. I told her to contact me in May when she comes to NY for a visit and we will catch up. She agreed and asked if I was happy. I told her I was, but honestly I'm not sure what she meant. Is anyone really happy? I asked her if she was still hitting the bottle and she said she was. I understand, I have been too. I told her that maybe she should lighten up a bit, knowing I would never. And then she started screaming that I was a hypocrite and hung up. I called her back the next day and apologized.

My intention was to tell her about my three day binge in Ohio over Christmas. She laughed at me Kim. And then asked if that was new. I asked her, "What's new?" She was right though the three day runs weren't uncommon for me. I explained to her that what was new was I usually remembered all three days, I blacked out on day one this time. I didn't even tell Herbert because he is already so worried about me. It really scared me Kim. Maybe I have that disease where you forget yourself and the things you have done. It certainly all points to it. I think I am going to go to the clinic to get checked. I hope I remember to go. Your mother was very kind to me and asked if I was mixing. I was, with junk but I told her with coke. Joyce accepted cocaine better than heroine. She hadn't touched it in years but was starting to mess with the pills. I told her it was all the same but she says no it's not. It is Kim. She was again kind to me and told me to clean up a little and get my focus back. I admitted to her that I needed a drink in the morning just to get going. I was surprised when she admitted to some days doing the same. She asked about Herbert as one does that understands he is my only family. I told her about his newest ventures and ours together. I was again surprised when she said, "You know you will be okay if something happens to Herbert." How does your mother know me so well? I was worried about such happenings to Herbert. We hung up on a good note and remembered that I've known her since 1967. I believe we are finally friends Kim.

Have the best year ahead.

Yours,

Louis

PS: Maybe I should have married your Mother.

Louie,

Hi, work has been so busy again. I had a patient last night that was crossing over to the other side and he said, "I can feel the warmth already, yes I'm ready." He held his arms up and then died. I believe in Gatekeepers and often wonder who yours was. I would like to think it was your biological mother, Nellie. Her and Charles were already regulars up there by the time you arrived. She loved her children so tragically. It would make sense it would be her.

I think back to the nineties and I was already working for a Cardiologist in Staten Island. I surrounded myself with people I wanted to be like in the nineties. Looking back it was a smart thing to do. I'm happy that you and Joyce stayed connected all those years after my birth. I know about the pills because my brothers told me. She wasn't good at hiding the fact she was high from them. I'm not sure which brother of the two told me that she would stay up all night cleaning, listening to music, and crash the day after. Sounded to me like a typical weekend on coke to me. But the younger one, Thomas, told me that she would take him to the doctor to get Adderall or Ritalin and take it for herself. He really sounded traumatized about that. I would have too, she was labeling him as a child with needs. I laughed when he told me that.

I'm not sure why.

On to the topic of you "blacking out." It's definitely the alcohol and drugs. You don't take her advice; you just keep on going at a fast pace. I'm off the next seven days and Brian and I are going away camping. I was told you loved camping.

I hate it. But it is certainly nice to be out and about again. Covid is slowly making an exit.

Louie,

Let's dive right into Joyce #2. I was so shocked to learn that you were married. Six months after I was born you married a girl named Joyce. She was a blonde beauty. Herbert introduced you to her at a party. And that's what the two of you had in common, partying. I found out about her via email from Laki. I printed out the pictures and wrote him back that it wasn't you. But it was you. I traced Joyce #2's email and found her. I called the number I found online. She answered and she was so surprised to hear from 'me.' I was surprised she knew about me. Joyce #2 didn't have anything positive to say about you. She told me you were an awful drunk. I had to remind her several times that they were twenty-years old when they married. She went on to say that she had to return to Virginia to get rid of you. I told her that these were the red flags of marrying a stranger after a night of partying. I didn't much enjoy the conversation with her.

Her voice was raspy and she had a recent stroke that left her speech impaired. I ended the conversation and wished her well. Two weeks later, she called me and told me she was in the hospital and they wouldn't let her out without having help. This lady wanted me to drive to Virginia and help her. So, I did.

10 hours later I was at the hospital signing paperwork. Joyce #2 told everyone we met that I was her daughter. She was no longer the blonde beauty that you had married. She was so thin and small. Several strokes left her weak. We filled out all the paperwork. We spent the week searching for Assisted Living homes. Joyce #2 had children of her own but two out of three died of an overdose. The third child didn't speak to her. I felt I had to help her but she was difficult and demanding. At the end of the week I moved her out of her trailer and into a really nice facility. I think it was the first time I saw Joyce #2 relax. I realized how scared she was entering this new phase of her life. I felt terrible for her, but I had to leave. I put money in her account and set up for wine and cigarettes to be delivered weekly. When I was leaving, she grabbed my hand and screeched, "Well at least something good came out of Louie." We spoke weekly. Seven months later I received a call that she passed away in her sleep. When they asked me what to do with her remains, I told them she had no funds and would be going to Potter's field in Fairfax Virginia. I never went back. I was glad she passed. Joyce #2

was finally free of the same demons you had. She had a tragic life, all due to drugs. I think meeting her made me realize that you were nowhere near being a father at age twenty. I think her part in this journey was to break the thought that maybe you could have raised me. You definitely could not have. Joyce #2 snapped me back into reality. I think of her from time to time. I think of her children that overdosed and thank God it wasn't me. It very well could have been. Most of your friends did well later in life but some did not. Joyce #2 couldn't straighten out even after being a mother. What a tragic story of your 'marriage.'   I'm off to the city tonight. Penny and I are meeting up with Edgar at the diner. I enjoy my time with the both of them. Penny and I are going on a road trip to Conneticut. I wish you could be joining us Louie.

Yours,

Kim

Letter # 12

Jan 17th, 1991

Kim,

I am on my way to Belgium but I had a dream last night. We were swimming in a lake in Upstate NY and we were splashing each other and having fun, the way I used to with my cousins back in Ohio. I was so happy to see you there with us. But then you disappeared in the water. I woke up and it felt very real. I was up journaling late into the night and I think that's what triggered the dream. I haven't thought of my cousins in a long time. I may give them a call. When we became teenagers we drifted apart. Family life at home became unbearable with Mom and Dad fighting all the time. There were no more family vacations or celebrations at the house anymore. Even now when I go I have to split my time between both families. Neither family understands me.

I lost so many friends in the last five years, it's hard to keep up. Life does that to you. You think all is good and then it all turns dark. I wonder about God and if he is real, the way he is described to be all-powerful. Why would he allow a disease to come and ravish the life of his followers? I haven't been back to church in a while. I no longer find the peace I once did now. I do believe in God though and I would have taught you the same. Today I plan on walking over to Tompkins Square Park and will write a few short stories. I need the money. Herbert has saved up enough for us until July. Things are getting harder for us to sustain. But Herbert never worries from day to day like I do. I can't imagine what I would be doing without him.

I hope you are well Kim. I will see your Mom next week in Brooklyn. Last we spoke she was doing well with the boys. I told her I see Halley all the time. She wants to meet her. I told her how much the two of you looked alike and I think I should not have said that. I haven't seen Halley for a few months now or longer. I showed your Mom her picture last time and she gasped at the likeness between you both. It is crazy though.

I actually do not think you received one letter but you may one day want to go to the Foundling and ask questions. The woman at the reception told me that they can't contact you. I don't see why not you are an adult now. There's no sense in asking more questions. I just hope they don't dump my letters in the garbage. It's all we have.

Yours,

Louis

PS: We launched air strikes against Iraq this morning. More blood is shed in the name of war.

Dear Louis,

I had such fun with my cousins growing up too. I told you Staten Island was a great place to grow up. I have cousins in Ohio too. Your nieces and nephew. They are the children of your half-sister that I don't care for. Imagine that I almost didn't respond to the oldest of the three, Susan. That would have been a loss for me if I didn't. This will sound strange but they are so normal it's crazy. Susan and I linked up on Ancestry and spoke on the phone for hours when we made the connection. Susan is the only one with your hair and it's hysterical. All three: Susan, Angela, and Dominic met me halfway between Ohio and New Jersey. We rented hotel rooms and went out for lunch, dinner, and cocktails. I want to be delicate in my description of them. Your half-sister was troubled while raising them. I'm not sure if troubled is even the word for it but she was real hard on them. I'm not going to go into too much detail because just like Kathy's daughter Tammy, it's not my story to tell but after meeting them I knew all my struggles in life were different from theirs and honestly I think theirs were worse. They came out on top though. The bond the three share is incredible. We are alike in many ways but I more think the likeness comes from the struggles of life more than the blood line. My meeting up with them was special because it was just us for the day. We all let our guards down and spilled our stories. We managed to cry and laugh and bond the way cousins should. I felt a pang in my heart when I left them. The second visit I met their partners and Angela's children. Louie, the level of beauty that runs in the family is astounding. I think Angela's daughter is the most beautiful girl inside and out. I'm not kidding when I say these are good people. A few months later Susan came to Jersey with her wife Maggie. I favor Maggie because you can tell she keeps the pieces together. She understands the bond the three have and embraces it with healthy boundaries.

Divorce is hard on the family unit. I think for adopted children it's harder. In your case it was. I was always grateful that my parents got along. They fought like all couples but it never lasted and the love never left them. My father still dates my mother. It's them against the world and always has been.

I'm sorry you went through that Louie.

When you died, your cousin's number was in your pocket. I always wondered about that. It was like you knew a next of kin would be needed. I mentioned that to Helen when I last visited her in Italy. Helen told me you did know. Two weeks before you died she read your cards and you pulled all three death cards and the violent death was shown to you. She said you laughed but knew it was coming. Did I tell you Helen lives in Italy now? I visit her often.

Let's just be grateful the letters were found and weren't thrown away. I have had to let it go that they weren't given to me at eighteen years of age. I truly believe you would not have been murdered and that's hard for my heart to carry. I also found a private investigator while my Joyce was still alive. He wanted two thousand dollars to tell me where she was, I didn't have the money at the time and missed her too. That also weighs me down. I have to trust in God that this all worked out the way it was supposed too. I too questioned my faith several times to date. Looking back it was always due to you and Joyce. I couldn't understand why he wouldn't want me with the two of you.

I was really lost in my twenties and doubted my faith but then I went to Portugal. I was in Lisbon and took a bus tour. We were passing a most beautiful sight of people crawling in white. I asked the tour what was happening and he casually said, "Oh that's the Fatima pilgrimage." I sat back down and thought and said to the others, "Why are we going to see a cork tree and not this?" I jumped back up and said, "Let me off." I got to the holy square and dropped to my knees and started crawling. I wasn't sure why. I prayed to get one of the beautifully dressed Cardinals or perhaps a Bishop. The heat was hot but I continued the crawl. There were mothers loudly praying for their sick children. I prayed with them, loudly. Strangers pinned wax fixtures on me to throw in the burning bush when I reached the altar. I pinned a wax heart on my white tee. Before I did I broke it in half. I carried my broken heart on my shoulder. Heat exhausted I reached the altar. I was so disappointed that I was next in line to be blessed by a nun. A meek, simply dressed Nun. I threw the wax parts in the burning bush and reached her feet. I didn't know how sad I was at that time because I always kept it in but on that day I didn't. I cried at her feet and she unpinned the broken wax heart from my shirt that I didn't realize I didn't throw in the bush and in broken english she asked why I was broken. I cried, "I'm so tired Sister, I can't find my parents, I don't feel loved." She pointed at the sky. I looked up and there were murals of two of the three shepherd children. Again, in broken english she said, "I am Sister Lucia, a shepherd child." I felt embarrassed. I knew the story of Fatima well. Why didn't I know she was still alive? Sr. Lucia held me in her arms and whispered in my ear that Mary the mother of God was my mother and all will come to light. We prayed for what seemed to be forever. She wiped my tears and kissed my forehead. I felt immense sadness when she passed away a few years later. I would have loved to return to her and tell her she was right and all did come to light and my heart is whole now.

Yours,

Kim

PS: September 11th, 2001 we were attacked on American soil. Worst day ever. "All gave some, some gave all." NY got hit so hard. Planes flew into the Twin Towers and we lost so many. God bless the FDNY and NYPD that were lost that day and God bless all today who still suffer from that day. The country wasn't prepared and the heroes went into the rubble to dig for bodies and weren't protected. The air quality was poor for months after. Now over twenty years later we are still losing lives from that attack. It could happen again today. You were right to worry about nuclear weapons, they are very much a reality in the world today. It's getting worse in the most recent years. We are going backwards and the hate towards others is appalling and sad. Life is a cycle for sure. When we learn to just live and let others do the same?

Letter # 13

December 8, 1991

Dear Kim,

You will be twenty-three this year. Today is my birthday and I almost forgot it. Herbert reminded me. I have a little money in the bank to get to Ohio. I have to renew some paperwork I have let slide. I'm not traveling in the year to come. Maybe a quick trip in the states but nothing abroad going on for me right now. I wonder if you travel, or if you have a 9-5 job, right here in the city.

Your Mom will be here in NY again in the summer. She's happy Kim.

I don't remember her this happy, ever. She has made herself a family. As she was telling me about the goings on of her life, I couldn't help but to wonder if she realized that she was glowing. I told her and she smiled and told me that I looked good too. I walked her back to her car and she asked me if I was ever going to change. I told her, "no." I don't need to change, I need a break.

I'm working on a few things here in NY with my friend Gregory. Gregory has introduced this guy to me who is interested in my short stories. Maybe I will make a small collection of all of my writings and get paid a heap of money. Herbert and I could use it.

Until then I have to make each cent I have count. If I had one birthday wish this year, I would close my eyes and when I opened them, you would be sitting across from me with your little sister. I really screwed up on so many levels. But I can't change the past, only the future. I wish you were present in my life. I sometimes think I made you up and you aren't real. You are like a figure of my imagination. The part of my mind that is good, I see you as being a beautiful young woman. Perhaps married. Or maybe you are still in the University studying to make a difference in the world. I think you are a strong female with your own opinions.

I spoke to my sister Kathy yesterday on the phone and when she knew it was me she told me that when I come back to Ohio she has so much to tell me. I wonder what any of that could be about. She also told me that she knows that our mother died. I first thought Marge but I had just spoken to that crazy broad, so Kathy meant our biological mother. I told her I didn't care if she was dead or alive. Kathy got mad and said, "well don't worry they are both dead." Then she hung up on me. But I really can't stop thinking about it. I might ring her again and ask for more details. She said our Mom's name was Nellie and our Father was named Charles but he was called 'Red.' I can't believe a father of mine had red hair. I told Kathy not to fall down some rabbit hole looking for redheads. I do think about them from time to time but to just drop your kids off to the church is a horrible thing to do. But then I remember you were in an orphanage too. If I ever told Kathy she would kill me. Kathy wants to see Halley and asked me to bring her when I come. I haven't seen Halley in a long time. I can't tell her that either. If I told Kathy that, she would say that Halley's mother is a smart woman. I hate her sometimes. But I really don't hate her. It really was the two of us for a long time. I had to protect her and was happy not to when we got adopted. Kathy says that she's not all that happy with her husband but she didn't elaborate. Money wise I think Kathy does well so maybe she shouldn't complain. I asked her if he was throwing her around because from what I see he does have a nasty temper. I never see her children anymore either. She told me that I have avoided all responsibilities in my life. That's not true. I have only escaped the miserable life she now lives. If I find out her husband hits her, I will kill him. She also told me that our 'parents' are aging and I never come around to help. I do what I can. She thinks I'm a "druggie" and that's it. She doesn't respect my art at all.

I will drop this letter off tomorrow and ask again how to find you, you are older and they should really allow some communication. The lady I usually speak to isn't there anymore. I think she retired. Maybe I will have better luck with the new lady in the front. Herbert and I are going to the Russian place tonight, at least he thinks my birthday is worth a celebration. Then we will walk over to the Chelsea to meet up with others. I'm forty-three now Kim and I don't feel a day older than a hundred.

Happy birthday baby,

Yours,

Louie

PS: The world is yours only for a moment, hang on for dear life.

Dear Louie,

The stack of letters you have written to me is getting down to the last few. I read them with caution. I know these last few letters will break my heart. You will only have a few more birthdays.

Kathy was obsessed with finding Nellie and Charles. But this is what confuses me and I never thought to ask her when she was still living, Kathy found them years before she told you about them. You saw her enough times that she should have told you. I think the only reason why she told you in 1991 was because, it's around this time that you will meet your half-sister. But that is confusing too because Kathy met her when she was in her twenties.

Kathy's husband did toss her around. He's not the father of her children, the father of her three kids was killed in a car accident when he was twenty-one. I know you know that but you never wrote about him. Kathy does divorce him and now the trauma bonds continue because her children don't know much about their father or his family either. Kathy was never financially secure until a little later in life. Louie, she worked hard her whole life and had a funny relationship with money. Kathy was cheap. No other way to put it but she had reason to be. Kathy thought like I do. We can only depend on ourselves for money. So we worked. I work hard too but I really love being a nurse so it rarely feels like work to me. To be honest, I look back to 1991 and I was so happy. The doctor and his family that I worked for were absolutely amazing. I was taught more about medicine than most nurses did over their whole career. The doctor was the one who told me to travel. He came from India and said traveling will be a whole different education for me.

He was right. When all my friends were getting married, I was dancing under the stars in Hungary. When they were getting divorced I was running naked at a carnival in Rio. I couldn't be tied down with relationships with men. I was free and planned to stay that way. I was catching flights not feelings. I was never afraid to hop on a plane and go to the places people only dreamed of going but fear held them back. Those were the days to do it. It was cheap then. Not anymore. But I'm still hopping on planes, now I hop on them with your friends. Halley, I think, has the travel gene in her too. I've been thinking about her a lot, I wish I would have handled things differently with her. But like you I can't change the past. I'm also doing the best I can.

You will return to Ohio and meet your half-sister and your brother Jim will join you with Kathy and it will be a great day for you. A great day for you all. I know this because when cleaning out Jeremiah's apartment I find an envelope with the pictures of that exact day. This now brings me to tell you something more about your half-sister. When you met her you were really impressed with her and she with you. At first when I found the photos I thought how wonderful it was that your day of revelation came. You finally found out your story.

But not only did I find the pictures, I bought a book called, 'The American Hipster.' I bought it because when I googled your name and the book came up. Firstly, I will say that it is an amazing book. Very well written about Herbert Huncke and the times it was written about. As I was reading it a part came up where you are mentioned. You are mentioned by your half-sister. She said that after you met you returned later on and showed up on her doorstep. She described you as dirty and foul smelling. She said you asked for help and she turned you away. Now that bothered me. But then I read she said that you turned away and had "soiled" your pants. Now understand that this lady has also written that she loved you so much and was so happy to have found her 'long lost brother.' Your half-sister was a nurse at the time and I will say that reading that took my breath away. How a nurse couldn't have helped you hurts my heart but to have your nurse sister turn you away broke my heart. I could and never will forgive that. When I told Penny, she laughed and said I have a "middleclass" reaction to that. Helen didn't seem bothered by it either but they both understood why it bothered me. You were weak when you went to her and you really needed the help. At least as a nurse she could have steered you in the right direction to get help if she couldn't do it. Can you imagine that this is the Aunt that Halley is in contact with? I also realize that having a junkie brother showing up can be scary but the nurse in me would have helped. I just think that your day was due. I have spent countless nights thinking of what if I found you? Would you still have died? I will never know. But what I do know is soiled pants or not I would have helped you. Shame on her.

I hope you enjoyed your birthday at the Russian restaurant. Oddly you will die in front of it in a few years. Ugh to know the things now that I didn't then was maybe a blessing.

Love you,

Kim

Letter # 14

June 6th 1992

My Dear Kim,

What is the true meaning of life? I don't ask this question lightly. Is it procreating? Is it working until you die? Why do we suffer so much? Is there an after-life? I can walk outside and see the beauty of the city, then walk over a block and see the chalk line of another victim that was shot or stabbed. I become overwhelmed with the amount of hate in the world. Herbert and I are doing the best we can to overcome and embrace new changes in our lives. Herbert is aging and although he doesn't slow in any way he is having a harder time to get going. This worries me. So many things these days worry me. I feel I am changing. I'm not as happy as I once was. I went home to Ohio again, and as always this proved to be a mistake. Why can't I go home without judgement? I feel sorry for them. They are caged up in lives they don't want to live in. I may be living my "gypsy, druggie, life" but Kim, I am free. I want you to feel the freedom I do. I lost so many friends in the last few years and the streets keep moving along as if they were never here. Is that how it will be when it's my time? Will I be forgotten as a man? What have I done that could be my legacy?

I called your Mom the other day just to catch up on her life. I needed a distraction from my own. She told me that she was home in Brooklyn again and it was a short visit so she didn't call but she saw a young girl on 86th street and thought it was you. I asked her what "you" looked like. She told me you were blonde with long wavy hair and you were small in stature. When she got closer she saw your blue eyes and looked away. Joyce said she got scared. She thought maybe she hallucinated the girl in her head. She turned away and didn't look back. I told her it's possible you could have been in Brooklyn, it could have been you. She said even if it was what would she say? She asked if I still write to you. I told her I did and asked if she wanted to include a letter. I was surprised when she said, "no." I didn't try to convince her to write you because I know you are getting these letters now. I continue to write you for me. It's therapeutic. I know I created you and your sister. Maybe you will both do something so great and that will be my legacy.

Herbert encourages me to keep writing to you but thinks I should write about you too. I don't share all the letters I write to you with him but the ones I have he always says, "Louis you lead your letters with passion, keep writing." Herbert understands me in ways my family never did. I know I repeatedly tell you this but find friends that become your family.

My friend David is really sick. He has AIDS and isn't getting better. More of his body is being ravaged and surrendering to this awful disease. When home I was telling my father about how bad it was and he asked if I was in physical contact with them. I'm not sure what he exactly meant by that but I told him I have kissed each one of them on and in the mouth. The look of horror on his face was telling. I will call his partner Tom in the late afternoon to see if I can go over to the Village and see them. And just like last week I will kiss him. I have confided in David about myself and my reasons for leaving Ohio. We have similar experiences and I consider him one of the best human beings I have ever been around.

Yours,

Louie

PS: Be careful out there Kim. Look for the beauty in life first and when you come to the ugly, and you want to give up, don't, close your eyes to all the beauty you have stored and keep moving. Move with the streets with caution, but keep moving.

Dear Louie,

Why do you keep going back to Ohio. Everytime you write that you do, I scream, "WHY are you back there?" You do tell so much to David. At Fales when I listened to your conversations with him, I wondered if you told Herbert some of the personal details about your teenage years the way you have told David. I feel the love you had for him. I also feel your sorrow in losing him this way. I wish I could hold you. It's terrible for me at times to know I comfort so many and never got the opportunity to comfort you.

I don't know what the end game or what the meaning of life is, but I see so much end of life that I know that we should all live as free as we can be. I do look at only the beauty. The ugly will drown me. I do keep it moving but not on the streets Louie. I keep to the grass, the side where the beauty is. The streets you refer to are filled with blood. I feel sometimes if you only crossed over to the grass you would not have drowned in the ugly. The older I get the more I realize that I know nothing more about life than I did when I was born.

For me, your legacy are these letters. Your truth in them. Your loyalty to Joyce warms my heart. Your loyalty to Herbert leaves me in awe. More of your legacy are your photographs. They have surfaced in the most impressive of places. But it's your ongoing commitment to me and for that you have made me whole. I walk in confidence now in a way I never did before. You did that for me. I love you Louie. That's your legacy.

The girl Joyce saw was not me unless she was in a bar late at night. In 1992 I was going to Brooklyn quite often bar hopping.

I feel like my life is changing too these days. I feel like Brian is pulling away from me. He has put up with so much of me for years. I have with him too but this is the first time that I feel like I might face my elderly years alone. I can and up right now, I am lucky to get a hello from him. I think he has checked out. I find myself these days looking for options for my future if I was to have one without him and none of the options I have come up with satisfy what I thought my ending would be like. I didn't want a long term relationship. I was engaged and broke it off and it had nothing to do with the man. I have never been in a relationship where my partner could not have provided me a good life, the problem has always been me. The life of feeling free that you talk of is my life. No man other than Brian has been able to provide that for me. I have wings with Brian. They were broken when we became lovers and he fixed them and let me fly. His wings were never broken, but I have never clipped them either. I am not naive enough to believe I would find that twice in my lifetime but maybe I don't need it either. I think that if Brian left me, I would stay alone and never settle for anything less than the flight Brian has given me. I can fly solo and that's what matters. I guess.

Love,

Kim

PS: You wrote this letter on the exact date you will die a year later. That's haunting and beautiful.

Letter # 15

July 23rd, 1992

Kim,

I've been ill with grief. David died yesterday. A part of me died too. David was more than my friend, he was my brother. We formed a friendship around the horrors we shared with another that blossomed into a perfect flower. In our later years of friendship we spoke on so many aspects of life and how we would navigate to the next decade. He was too young at thirty-seven to leave me behind here with plans that will never come to light for a decade ahead that he will not be a part of.

That's all I have for today Kim. I'm sorry. Today my streets feel abandoned.

Yours,

Louis

PS: I'm trying to find the beauty, when I close my eyes I see You

My dear Louie,

I am so sorry for the loss of your friend David. He will live on for years to come and through him you will too. hope when it is my time to reach you I meet him and thank him for not only for what he has done for you but for me. Rest in divine peace

David Wojnarowicz

September 14, 1954 - July 22nd, 1992

Yours,

Kim

PS: I'm closing my eyes and seeing you both in heavenly love.

Letter #16

September 1992

Dear Kim,

I'm hanging in there these days. I have good days and bad ones since I lost David. I don't go on about it to anyone because I don't think anyone would understand how sad I am over his death. I am really worried about Herbert. I don't know what I would do if I lost him. Herbert is very important to so many people but not like he is to me. I tell him I'm worried and he worries along with me and about me too. The other day in conversation he asked me if I would change anything and honestly I wouldn't except for you. I am really missing Helen these days too. She is away right now and I can't wait for her to come back so we could drink wine and laugh together. That's the thing about Helen, she is always happy. When I see her I smile and my whole world gets better. I haven't written anything lately, I just don't have it in me right now. I feel tired all the time these days. I lost some weight but I really haven't been eating all that much either.

I have been working on a few projects with Allen and I hope it leads to somewhere. It's getting expensive to develop my negatives. I did go back to Social Security but they said my case is pending. I don't know how long all of this will take.

I hope you are doing well and enjoying yourself. At 24 I can only imagine what you are up to. I was hoping to have already known you Kim.

I have a friend Gregory that is going to be staying with us for a few nights so I know my spirits will be lifted soon, then Helen will be back. I don't expect that I will be feeling this down for long. It's not my usual way to be. I think I am easy going, but life has been real cruel to me lately.

I called your Mom the other day but I didn't leave a message. I just wanted to say hello to her, I thought may be that would cheer me up. She must have been out with the kids. I will try again next week. More soon.

Yours,

Louie

PS: My favorite color is red. What's your's kiddo?

My Dear Louie,

The loss of a friend is never easy. I feel your pain but as we both know you will see David again sooner than you think. I wonder if the friend you mention is Gregory Corso. I found so many pictures of him on the negatives that you could not afford to get developed.

I have a story to tell you about Gregory's daughter, Sheri. Your friend Laki told me to contact her and I did on Facebook. She called me not long after I messaged her. I believe we were on the phone for a few hours. Her life story is incredible. She found out Gregory was her Dad and met him and they had a beautiful relationship. She cared for him in his last days on this earth. She also found all of her siblings and has remained close to them. I think she should write a book. Sheri is a nurse like myself. I had so many questions and she answered them all.

I haven't met Sheri in person but I plan to soon now that Covid restrictions have been completely lifted. I got Covid in the beginning of the year. I felt as if every bone in my body was breaking but a week later I was fine. I am one of the lucky ones. Brian had it too and is okay as well. Maybe you were watching over us. Brian's dad died a few years ago and he is really missed. He also grew up an orphan. He made a family with the love of his life and had seven children. One sadly passed, I think at birth. But he raised his six children and took care of his family. I'm not comparing you to him or to my father, it's just that sometimes I think you could have made some sacrifices for me. I understand in the beginning the age difference between you and Joyce limited you but then you had Halley and I would have thought that your 'Dad' game would have been stronger. At least with her.

I'm leaving for Italy in an hour. I'm going to spend the week with Helen. We have truly formed the most beautiful relationship over these last couple of years. I am so tired from working all of the time but Brian and I are still going through this rough patch. When I get nervous I work and Brian is making me nervous as he pulls further and further away from me. When Helen and I get to Rome I will throw my coin into the Trevi Fountain and make my wish for us to reconnect or separate but the waiting around for things to improve is torture.

Did I tell you that I found Robbie? Robbie Huncke. She is the niece of Herbert. I think Robbie, Sheri, and myself need to all get together and hug each other. It should be in NY too. I am going to work on setting that up. Have to run. I hope your day got better.

Yours,

Kim

PS: I don't have a favorite color. This month I like neon orange. Just got the cutest heels and bag to match in orange.

Letter # 17

January 11th 1993,

Kim,

I meant to write you on your birthday Kim but time has been escaping me these days. I really need this Social Security to come through. I will get a check and I think I can get some money for Halley too. I had to go to Ohio again for all of this and I can't afford to go back and forth anymore. I told my Grandmother I would mow the lawn and clean up her yard for a few bucks. After I was done she didn't pay me and I had to wire Herbert to send me money for cigarettes. I am really tired of living with no money at all. I'm not writing anymore other than to you and I'm not sure if I should even continue to do even that. I spoke to your Mother and told her that we could join a registry where adopted children register to find their parents. I've been going to the library and learning how to use the computers there. I think by joining the group it will give us a better chance on reuniting. Joyce as usual says, "No." We spoke last on your birthday. It was your twenty fifth. She is right if you haven't come for us by now you may never come.

I saw my sister Kathy while in Ohio. She gained a little weight but it looked real good on her and when I told her she flipped out on me. I will never mention weight again around her. Melvin had pictures of her kids up and Kathy did good with them. All good looking kids. But Kathy never looks happy ever. It doesn't matter what is going on, the fact that I breathe sends her through the loops of hate. I really try and joke with her but she's not fun at all. That brings me to your Mom when I saw her last she put on weight too. I was going to say how good she looked but when I slapped her thigh she looked at me with death in her eyes and said, "You mention my weight and I will stab you." She held her key up as to assure me I would be stabbed with the key. I laughed so hard until she laughed. Our relationship is great at the moment. Actually it's been great for a few years. I was never in love with your Mom, Kim. Not in the way I was with Rosa or am with Helen. But Joyce and I share you. I love her differently. I hope you know love Kim. The kind that doesn't crumble under pressure or deceit.

Yours,

Louie

PS: I told Joyce when you were born that you were going to be very special. I hope that spirit that you had that made your eyes glow didn't get broken. That would kill me if we locked eyes again and that spark was gone.

Louis,

I stopped writing for a few months. My administrator of the company I work for is not feeling well. She's sick. I am so busy trying to see her and do what I can for her and I'm still working crazy hours. I got back from Italy and had the most restful time with Helen and her partner Marco. Marco is a bit controlling with the time we should be doing everything in. I write this while laughing. At one point in the day he would tell me it's time to rest and I would. I love them together. He is so gentle with her and treats her with such love and respect. I worry about his health though. His blood pressure is really high and I told him the medicine he is taking is making it worse. Helen said she would bring him back to the doctors. Helen and I have planned a trip to Paris in a few months from today and I am really excited to be going back to France. I have nothing but the best memories from my visit there with the doctors.

When I got back Brian seemed to be more talkative and interested in how my trip was. Maybe the Trevi Fountain is magical. My first wish there was decades ago. Of course I asked to find you two. I should have wished for you to be alive, but I did find you. So there's the proof the Trevi is magical. Maybe, I will be granted another.

I don't think Joyce was in love with you either. But I know she loved you because she would not have kept in touch with you otherwise. I totally just made that up Louie; I actually have no idea. But it never sounded like a love story. I mentioned Dean Lance in earlier letters he told me about you and Rosa and honestly it did sound like you were in love with her but reality takes over and money is important to raise a child. I'm not sure what happened between the two of you. I just heard it was ugly in the end. You told me about Helen. I found a small book of your love for Helen. I gave it to her. But that's how I knew you fell mad for her. I like that she was your last love. As I have said before Helen is easy to be around. We spoke of you and she told me that a few weeks before you died she read your cards and you pulled all death cards. She was convinced that you knew you were going to die. Your response was that you wanted it to be quick and painless. I just adore Helen.

I joined that registry too, got nowhere. I would not have been looking for Cartwright.

Yours,

Kim

PS: I think you are the only one who saw the spark. I have more of a touch than a spark in my eye.

Letter # 18

April 12th, 1993

Dearest Kim,

I am writing and creating again. I was able to get off the junk for a while now. I'm just smoking a few joints a day and drinking only after 3 pm. I feel stronger than I have been in a while. Herbert is slowing down on traveling for a bit. He's aging in body but not in his mind. My body and mind are both declining. I am tired all of the time, and can't keep anything down for a while now. But today I feel better. I left the city early this morning to photograph the Brooklyn Bridge. I want to capture all the seasons of the bridge. My winter shot came out really good. The cover photo I did for Herbert's book is really good too. Maybe my time is coming although I feel death all around me. It's almost as if I am being pulled away to the other side. I keep dreaming that I am packing for a trip but when I get to the airport, I am not allowed to bring my bags. I get on the plane and I see others like me without bags. Faces are blank. I always wake up right before we land.

Herbert and I are making plans to go back to Belgium. You know Kim, I have been judged by many people and really don't care but I would care what my girls would think of me.

I want you to always know that you are thought of. These letters are what I have for you. I wish you could know the people I know. Walk on the same street as me. Only then you would understand the sacrifices I made to live the life I wanted. I'm not saying this is the life for anyone else but again, I tell you, I have lived a free life doing what I had to do to remain free.

I have made a decision not to return to Ohio again. I have had it being in places where my art or my life goes unappreciated. I have accepted the fact that I am not wanted there or needed there. Everyone has made their families and lives and I am not included in anything. The worst feeling ever is to be standing in places that you are not wanted. I hope never to see Kathy again. My job as her older brother is over. She has made that clear to me that she does not need a "druggie" in her life. Her kids are grown and I hardly know them. I hardly know her. I hope you have had better siblings than I did.

Be well Kim. Be kind always and remember that you don't always know what someone else is going through. You are most likely raising your own family now. Or falling in love. As much as falling in love feels wonderful it also feels awful when it dies. Don't let that ever get to you there will always be people to love. Love freely regardless of gender. Let others live despite the bullshit religious leaders may tell you.

Love is the universal sign of God. It doesn't matter which God you believe in, they all count. Don't ever let a man abuse your mind or your body. Just being alive is reason enough to leave an abuser. Never stay in a relationship where there are no meaningful words or conversation. Don't ever stay at a job that is robbing you of life. Balance is key. I love you Kim. I didn't try hard enough, I didn't run after the car that day because I was scared. Scared that I wasn't good enough to raise you. Scared I would place you in the wrong directions in life. I was scared your mother would fail and I would have to raise you alone and give up my life. I wish things turned out differently for us. I will look for you in all the other worlds I will travel until we are finally together. Maybe next life you will be my mother and pardon me for the failure of a father that I was and take pity on me and love me unconditionally. Am I that bold to ask forgiveness to a child that I failed? I am. Forgive me, Kim. Forgive your mother, she did what she thought was best for you. Perhaps we were selfish and kept you too long, long enough to remember you were given away. For that I am truly sorry.

I used to wish that if you came back you would tell me that you remembered us and never forgot the love we gave you for a limited time. That it carried you through your darkest hours. Now I wish for a different outcome. I wish for you to return and tell me you were a princess and spoiled beyond belief. I wish for you to look at me and spit on the ground and tell me you are nothing like me. Then I want for you to walk away and never look back. Be like the streets and keep moving. The world is moving at a fast pace and computers will take over, don't let it. Touch the people you love. Tell them often that you love them. And most importantly Kim, let others love you. This is an area where I am at fault. I would rather feel unloved because it's my safe place if that makes any sense at all.

Yours,

Louis

PS: I think I have Hepatitis, I tested negative for HIV but something isn't right. I have become careless in my days of despair. Honestly, I don't care if I live or die anymore. Maybe in my next life, just maybe, I will be…. Happy.

Dearest Louis,

Don't give up. Go to the Methadone clinic with Herbert. Get help. I know the ending but perhaps we are living side by side in present time. Maybe tonight when I sleep I will wake up Kim Indrieri Cartwright and save you. I need to save you Louis. Let me love you. If it is true that we will travel again together I will love you with the unconditional love you deserve. Don't let the devil win Louie.

It was you Louie who made me whole again. Your letters to me are the best part of us both. You were a child when I came into this world, I understand you couldn't do it. I am sorry I didn't find you sooner despite what people may say. Perhaps, I could have helped you heal in ways others couldn't help you. I wish Halley would allow me in her life but if it never comes to light I am grateful to know the truth that she exists and is thriving.

I want so badly to run back to the Cardinals and tell them I just didn't understand what was happening. I'm sorry that I couldn't see the light sooner. In a perfect world I would have found you. If it was meant to be it would have happened. I believe that now. I feel your love and your desperation to make it all right. It's okay, Louie. I forgive you.

It's almost time to say goodbye Louie. I don't want to.

I find comfort in knowing that I will always have these letters. Letters From The Grave.

I am leaving for Paris tomorrow to meet Helen. We are going to live for you Louie. We will toast your life and how you lived it. Without the shame you think you have brought to me. I know you now Louie, I know you are smart and loving, and kind. You can rest easy now Louie. You belong to me and I you. That will never change.

Yours,

Kim

PS: You do have Hepatits. A,B and C. Trust me, being stabbed to death was better.

Louie,

I am in France rerouting to Italy. Helen's partner Marco has died suddenly. I will be with her to get her through this awful loss. Edgar will join us tomorrow. Please watch over her until I get there.

Louie,

I am in Italy and Helen is heartbroken. I want to take her away from Tarquinia and go to Rome where she can breathe. We are waiting for Edgar and will go after we see Marco off at his burial. I am so sad he passed. He loved Helen. But now he joins you and Harvey. Take care of him; he, like you, is tough on the outside but so gentle within. Watch over us more than ever.

Louie,

My time in Italy is ending, I have to return to the States for work. I will come back in a few weeks to be with Helen again. Edgar will stay in the meantime. We felt you in Rome. I feel you now. Thank you for getting us through this week.

Louie,

I'm home. I made more wishes at the Trevi. Please see them through. So far the Trevi has not disappointed me. My mentor, administrator, and friend is free from the disease that could have ended her life. I'm looking for all the beauty these days.

Yours,

Kim

Letter # 20

May 28th, 1994

Kim,

It is with great heartache that I tell you I will be homeless in a few days. You won't be able to find me at the location I gave to you before. This is your Mother's number

I will keep in touch with her so that if you do come you have an idea where I will be. I am going to go to a shelter in Chinatown for now until I can figure out what to do. Herbert is at the Chelsea. At least he is safe.

I am not sure what will become of me. You may be walking in the city and see me lying in the street. If you recognize me, don't stop. Let your Mother tell you about me and who I used to be, not what I have become.

I don't know how long I will be on the street. I have sold everything I could to eat for the next few days, but after that I am not sure what will happen. I am alone.

I am going to sleep and if there is a God I will not wake up. Please know I tried to stay clean. I tried to stop it all, but it has become stronger than I am. I can't afford a ticket back to Ohio and I feel too weak to even travel back. This might be my last letter to you for a while. I will write again when I am set up some place else.

I called your Mother and she told me to get to Virginia. I can stay with her friend but I can't even get the energy to go. I can't leave Herbert right now either.

I feel like I am going crazy in the head. My thoughts aren't right. I have done terrible things in the last few weeks, Kim.

My mother, Nellie, is not dead Kim. I saw her. I have been lied to. When I reached out to her she slapped me. I told her I would get better but she came to me in the night and told me to follow her. I am going to go with her if I see her again. There is a war happening outside of my apartment. I hear the shots fired, animals are being killed. It's raining blood from the sky. I think the world is ending, I know mine is. I have to find Herbert or Allen. I haven't seen either one of them in weeks. Maybe Laki knows where they are. I should phone him but I don't have a phone. I will try to write again soon to you.

Your Father,

Louis Roy Cartwright

Oh Louie,

Why didn't you go to Chinatown? Why did you go to the church? Your Mother Nellie is not alive Louie. You were not lied to. There is no war outside. You are hallucinating. I feel so helpless. The tears are flooding my vision. I can hardly write this letter. Why didn't you go to the hospital?

You are right, your life is ending and I can't stop it. I am too late. Oh Louie why didn't I push harder to find you. I am so sorry. I can only find comfort in knowing your death will be quick. Go to Nellie, Louie. Call out for her. She is your Gatekeeper. Take her hand and go into the night with her. It's your time. Don't be scared my love. Go where you feel the love and warmth. Don't worry about Herbert, he will join you soon. You will have eternity together. You lived your life the way you wanted, have no regret.

I am going to the things you couldn't. I will live free and have only peace in my life. I will let others love me. I will continue to be in the service of others and will continue to travel. To the places you have walked and to the places you haven't. I will wait for Halley and if she ever needs me, I will be there. I promise you Louie! Go in peace. Kiss my Grandmother for me. Tell her Susan, Dominic, Angela, Tammy, and Rick all love her. Keep Michael close to you. Forgive your sister, she forgave you. Start over where there is no judgement or sadness. Start over heroine and drug free.

Let God love you Louie. When I see you again it will be on my deathbed and when you hold your hand out, I will grab on and go with you. Forgive yourself.

I love you forever and a day.

Your Daughter

PS: My name is Marie.

September 9th 1994

Hi Kim,

I am writing to you to tell you that your Father Louis Cartwright died on June 6th, 1994. My name is Joyce Indrieri Mooney. I am your Mother. Your biological mother. Your father has written you many letters, I am not sure that you have ever received them or if he ever dropped them off to the Foundling. But in the case that he did, I wanted you to know that the reasons the letters have stopped is because he died. He was murdered. When I received the call from Herbert he was just as surprised as I was. Louie was not the type of person anyone would want to hurt. He was a handful but was a good person with his own demons. I have enclosed my number and address if you receive this and want to contact me. You also have a sister and two brothers. I gave your sister up for adoption like I did with you. I married and have two boys. You are very much a part of us.

Please thank your parents for taking you in when I couldn't keep you. I hope life is kind to you. You were a very happy baby and smart as a whip. You were walking before you were a year old, you loved bananas and cream. The greatest joy I have ever felt was your touch. Know that you were given up for a better life. Not because you weren't loved.

Love,
Joyce

Dear Joyce....

The end

goodbye . . ?
oh no, please. Can't

we go back to page one

and do it all over
again?

-Winnie The Pooh

Herbert Huncke by Louis Cartwright late 1970s

About the Author

Marie Cardinal

Marie Cardinal is a Registered Nurse practicing in Ocean County New Jersey as a Hospice Nurse and resides in Brick, New Jersey with her partner, Brian Sweeney.

Letters From The Grave

Marie Cardinal

&

Louis Cartwright

cover:
Regina Bartkoff

Back cover:
Louis Cartwright by Helen Oliver

photos:
Louis Cartwright

introduction:
Herbert Huncke

edit & layout: Aaron Howard

Made in the USA
Middletown, DE
03 September 2024

60220174R00071